Save Our Earth

Primary

Save time and energy planning thematic units with this comprehensive resource. We've searched the 1991–1997 issues of **The MAILBOX**® and **Teacher's Helper**® magazines to find the best ideas for you to use when teaching a thematic unit on the environment. Included in this book are favorite units from the magazines, single ideas to extend a unit, and a variety of reproducible activities. Pick and choose from these activities to develop your own complete unit or to simply enhance your current lesson plans. You're sure to find everything you need right here in this book to create a world of integrated learning experiences for your students.

Editors:
Kimberly Fields
Karen A. Brudnak

Artist:
Teresa R. Davidson

Cover Artist:
Kimberly Richard

www.themailbox.com

©1999 by THE EDUCATION CENTER, INC.
All rights reserved.
ISBN# 1-56234-335-1

Manufactured in the United States
10 9 8 7 6 5 4 3 2

Table Of Contents

Thematic Units

More Activities And Ideas

Reproducible Activities

Thematic Units...

from The MAILBOX® magazine.

Taking Care Of The Earth

A little tender loving care *can* make a difference for our Earth. In this unit you'll [find] practical ideas and activities to increase your students' environmental awarenes[s] and to help start or expand your own classroom recycling program. In no time a[t all] your students will see that their efforts really can help improve the environment.

ideas by Lori Bru[...]

Tender Loving Care

Encourage students to take an interest in their environment by having them "adopt" small areas of the school grounds for the entire school year. Divide students into small groups. Assign each group a designated area (approximately nine square yards). Have each group indicate the boundaries of its area with rocks, sticks, or other natural materials. Throughout the year, have students plan and carry out activities to show they care for the Earth. Activities may include cleaning up litter and debris, planting bulbs, placing homemade bird feeders in trees, and planting grass or flowers. Every time a group works in its area, photograph the activity. Display the photos on a bulletin board or in a photo album entitled "We Take Care Of The Earth." At the end of the year, students will be able to see that a little extra care goes a long way toward making the Earth a better place.

Mini-Landfills

Creating a mini-landfill gives students a firsthand look at the decomposing and biodegrading of various kinds of trash. For an outdoor landfill, obtain permission to dig a one-foot-deep hole on the school grounds. Have students bury the following items: several leaves (from trees or produce), apple wedges, strips of newspaper, a crushed aluminum can, and pieces of a Styrofoam® meat tray and a two-liter soft drink bottle. Then mark the mini-landfill site. Or create a classroom landfill by burying similar items in a large glass or clear plastic jar and sprinkling the soil with water every week. Each month, unearth the contents of your mini-landfill, noting any changes in a class journal. At the end of the year, dig up the items that did not decompose and recycle them.
Kimberly Spring—Gr. 2
Lowell Elementary, Everett, WA

We "Can" Do!

Americans use about 80 billion aluminum cans a year! Aluminum cans can be recycled over and ov[er] again. Use the reproducible on p[age] to introduce students to the proce[ss] of recycling aluminum cans. As a follow-up activity, set a class colle[c]tion goal; then have students col[lect] aluminum cans for recycling. Enl[arge,] color, and cut out the Earth Man [pat]tern on page 9. Display the cutou[t] with a class graph (see illustratio[n] entitled "We 'Can' Do!" Each wee[k] update the graph; then arrange f[or] an adult volunteer to take the ca[ns] to a local recycling facility. When [the] goal is reached, use any profits g[en]erated to purchase recycling rec[ep]tacles or plants for your school.

We "Can" Do

Our Goal | 250 ca[ns]

Number of Cans
(y-axis: 0, 50, 100, 150, 200, 250)

Number of Weeks
(x-axis: 1, 2, 3, 4, 5, 6, 7, 8)

Katie and Tyler pick up trash.

Ethan hangs a bird feeder

Plastic Tactics

...any types of plastics can now be recycled. To make identifying different ...s easier, numbers are imprinted on the bottoms of many plastic con- ...ers. Each number represents a different type of plastic. Have students ...tribute plastic items such as two-liter soft drink bottles; milk jugs; peanut ...er jars; butter and margarine tubs; and detergent, shampoo, and ...king oil bottles. Then have students sort the plastic containers using the ...mber imprints. Refer to the chart shown to identify the types of plastic ...ected. Check local recycling centers to determine which types of plastic ...accepted for recycling in your area. Recycle what you can, saving the ...recyclable plastics to use for arts-and-crafts projects and storage of ...sroom materials.

Code	Name of Plastic	Abbreviation	Common Items
1	polyethylene terephthalate	PET	soft-drink bottles, peanut butter jars
2	high-density polyethylene	HDPE	milk jugs, butter tubs, detergent bottles
3	polyvinyl chloride	PVC	water, shampoo, and cooking oil bottles
4	low-density polyethylene	LDPE	plastic grocery bags, some plastic wraps
5	polypropylene		plastic bottle caps, straws, and lids
6	polystyrene		yogurt containers, Styrofoam® products

300
250
200
150
100
50
0

Our Goal
300
newspapers

Pam Crane

Stamping Out Styrofoam®

Polystyrene foam, or Styrofoam®, is completely nonbiodegradable. Foam products buried in a landfill today will still be there 500 years from now! Have students bring in a variety of Styrofoam containers. Display the items; then, as a group, brainstorm alternative items that could be used in place of each of the containers. As a follow-up activity, duplicate student copies of the "Earth Gram" telegram on page 9. Ask some students to write and send telegrams to companies which use Styrofoam packaging, encouraging them to consider alternative packaging. Other students may send telegrams to companies that already use alternative packaging, expressing gratitude for their environmental awareness. "Telegram for Burger World!"

Save Our Trees

Every week Americans throw away the equivalent of about 500,000 trees in the form of newsprint. But recycling newspapers can help save trees. To reduce the amount of newspaper that is thrown away, start a classroom newspaper recycling center. (Before having students bring in newspapers, check your local fire code to see if the papers you collect must be kept in special containers.)

To create a motivational display, enlarge, color, and cut out the Earth Man pattern on page 9. Display Earth Man along with a large tree cutout bearing the caption "We're Saving Trees!" Have students help you set a class goal. Each week update the display; then have an adult volunteer take the newspapers to a recycling center. When the class goal is reached, have students make their own version of recycled paper by following the directions in *50 Simple Things Kids Can Do To Save The Earth* (Earthworks Group).

The Ream Team

The paper that four people use in a year weighs about as much as a big ca
Students can reduce the amount of paper they use at school by becoming
members of Earth Man's Ream Team. Have students brainstorm a list of way
reduce the amount of paper they use, such as completing several assignmen
on the same sheet of paper or using the back of each sheet of paper before
throwing it away. Then have students create their own Ream Team posters.

To create a poster, duplicate on white construction paper a copy of the Ear
Man pattern (page 9) for each student. Have each student color and cut out h
Earth Man pattern, before mounting it on the unprinted side of a cereal box
panel. Have him add a paper-recycling slogan or reminder, then display his
poster in a prominent place. A message from Earth Man will help everyone
remember to think twice before throwing away paper.

Trash Busters

To help reduce the amount of trash your class creates in the school cafeteria, sponsor class "trash-buster" days. On these days, have students drink milk without using straws and use cloth napkins instead of paper ones. To create a set of cloth napkins, have students fringe 12" squares of lightly colored, cotton fabric. If desired, use fabric crayons to decorate the napkins with recycling messages and illustrations. For each student who wishes to write a message on his napkin, have the student write his message on a separate sheet of paper. Trace the words on the *back side* of the paper with fabric crayon, and iron this inverted lettering onto the napkin. After each use, have a parent volunteer wash the napkins and return them to school. Other classes may follow your lead, and, with a little help from the cafeteria manager, you may even be able to sponsor schoolwide, trash-buster days!

Friends Of The Earth

Caring for the Earth is an ongoin
project. Prior to the first day of eac
month, duplicate a copy of the Frie
Of The Earth Calendar on page 8.
in the upcoming month and dates
before duplicating a copy for each
student. Have each student take h
calendar home and fill it in using th
code. At the end of each month, h
students return their calendars and
discuss the things they did to help
save the Earth. To recognize each
student's contributions, duplicate a
fill out a copy of the Friend Of The
Earth award on page 9 for each
student.

Toy-Consumer Savvy

Students are often enticed to purchase toys because of attractive packaging and advertising. Have students brainstorm a list of toys they recently received as gifts, bought with their allowances, or are considering buying. Discuss the toys and their packaging. Is the toy packaged in unnecessary materials? What happens to the packaging materials after the toy is opened? Is the toy durable? Is its package misleading? After the discussion, brainstorm a list of things smart junior consumers should consider before buying toys.

To encourage students to recycle their toys, hold a toy trade. Have each child bring in a toy he no longer wants or uses. Display the toys on a table. Place each child's name in a container; then randomly draw out the names. When his name is drawn, allow each child to select a "new" toy from the table.

Answer Key For Page 7

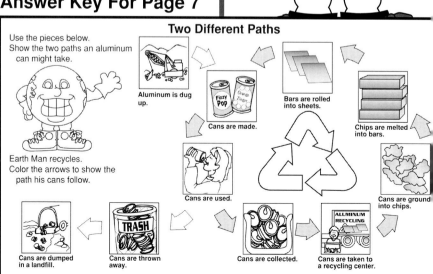

Two Different Paths

Use the pieces below. Show the two paths an aluminum can might take.

Aluminum is dug up.

Cans are made.

Bars are rolled into sheets.

Chips are melted into bars.

Earth Man recycles. Color the arrows to show the path his cans follow.

Cans are used.

Cans are ground into chips.

Cans are dumped in a landfill.

Cans are thrown away.

Cans are collected.

Cans are taken to a recycling center.

Two Different Paths

Use the pieces below.
Show the two paths an aluminum can might take.

Earth Man recycles.
Color the arrows to show the path his cans follow.

Aluminum is dug up.

Cans are made.

Bars are rolled into sheets.

Chips are melted into bars.

Cans are ground into chips.

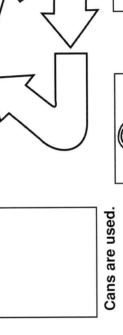

Cans are taken to a recycling center.

Cans are collected.

Cans are used.

Cans are thrown away.

Cans are dumped in a landfill.

Color.
Cut and paste.

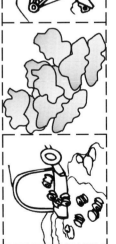

Friend Of The Earth Calendar

_____'s

Be a friend of the Earth!
Recycle paper, plastic, and cans.
Reuse trash you can't recycle.
Reduce the amount of trash you throw away.
<u>**Care**</u> for the Earth—pick up trash or plant growing things.

month _____

Sunday	Monday	Tuesday	Wednesday	Thursday	Friday	Saturday

Each day, do something to show you are a friend of the Earth.
Use the code to mark what you do on the calendar.

Code	
recycle trash	= ↻
reuse trash	= ↺
reduce trash	= →
care for the Earth	= ♡

Bonus Box: On the back of this sheet, draw and color yourself doing something you did during the month to care for the Earth.

©The Education Center, Inc. • Save Our Earth • Primary • TEC3178

Note To Teacher: Use with "Friends Of The Earth" on page 6

Earth Man Pattern
Use with "We 'Can' Do" on page 4, "Save Our Trees" on page 5, and "The Ream Team" on page 6.

_____

is a

Friend of the Earth

because _____

_____

_____

Keep up the good work!

date: _____

signed: ___Earth Man___

Use with "Stamping Out Styrofoam®" on page 5 and for additional correspondence as needed.

Earth Gram ☆☆☆☆☆

to: _____

from: Earth Man and _____

date: _____

_____

_____

_____

_____

_____

_____

_____

_____

A Pocketful Of Science

Trash Busters!

Throughout the world, a billion tons of garbage is produced each year. What can be done? Use these activities to show students how they can make a difference!

ideas by Ann Flagg

Activity 1: What A Waste!

You will need:

In a paper lunch sack
— an apple
— a few carrot sticks in a plastic sandwich bag
— a single-serving bag of chips
— a prepackaged fruit or pudding snack cup
— a sandwich in a plastic sandwich bag
— a paper napkin
a can of soda

What to do:

Right before lunch, show students the lunch you have packed (the items listed above). Then after lunch show them what remains of your lunch. Present these leftovers: a chunk of apple, a carrot stick, some bread crust, the empty snack cup and chip bag, two sandwich bags, the empty soda can, the paper napkin, and the lunch sack. (Save these leftovers for Activity 2.)

Questions to ask:

1. What purpose did most of the leftover items originally serve?
2. How could I reduce the amount of waste in my lunch tomorrow?
3. What did you throw away from your lunches today?
4. How could you reduce the amount of waste in your lunches tomorrow?

This is why:

Garbage, or solid waste, is defined as unwanted or useless material. Each person in the United States produces about three to four pounds of garbage per day! That means in one year one person creates over 1,000 pounds of garbage! However, much of this waste is not really garbage. Many items that land in the garbage could be reused or recycled. To reduce the amount of garbage in the United States, each person must learn how to decrease the amount of garbage he or she produces.

Activity 2: Where Does It Go?

You will need:

two clean, three-liter plastic soda bottles
moist potting soil
fine-tipped marker
spoon
scissors
two large self-sticking labels
leftovers from Activity 1

In advance:

Remove the label and base from each bottle; then cut away the top half of each bottle. Lightly pack soil into each container (about half full). Save the base of each bottle.

What to do:

Display the leftovers from Activity 1. Explain that there are two kinds of garbage—natural garbage and man-made garbage. Enlist your students' help in sorting the leftovers into these two groups. (If students can't decide, put a small piece of the garbage in each pile.) Inform students that most garbage is buried in landfills and show them the two mini-landfills you prepared. Designate one landfill for each kind of garbage and create a label for each one that includes the garbage samples that will be buried there. Attach the labels. Bury samples of each item. For the soda can, remove the tab and bury it. Seal each mini-landfill by fastening a bottle base to the top of each project. Two weeks later dig up the garbage for evaluation. Repeat in two more weeks.

Question to ask:

1. What do you think will happen to the man-made garbage? The natural garbage?

This is why:

There are three main ways to dispose of solid waste: land disposal, incineration, *and* recycling and waste reduction. *Much garbage ends up being buried in landfills. Burying garbage takes up a lot of space. In the mini-landfills, students will observe the food (natural garbage) beginning to decompose, or it may have rotted away altogether because it is* biodegradable. *Since man-made garbage decomposes at a much slower rate (if at all), students will observe minimal change in this mini-landfill. Much of the garbage thrown away each week is man-made. People must find ways to decrease man-made garbage. One way is to reuse and recycle as much as possible.*

Activity 3: Making Choices

You will need:
— **for half of your students**
  individual servings of prepackaged pudding, milk
  washable bowls (nonbreakable), spoons
— **for half of your students**
  ready-made pudding snacks in plastic containers
  disposable spoons

  measuring cup   access to a refrigerator
  two clear trash bags   cloth dish towel
  dishpan, dish soap, sponge,
    and water for washing dishes

What to do:
   Divide the class into two groups. Distribute the washable bowls and spoons to one group. Into each bowl measure the amount of instant pudding and milk needed to make a serving of pudding. Have the students stir the pudding as directed on the container, then refrigerate the pudding for five minutes. Next distribute the prepackaged pudding and disposable spoons to the second group. Talk about the time involved in preparing the two kinds of pudding. Retrieve the instant pudding from the refrigerator and let all students eat their pudding snacks. Then ask one student from each group to collect his group's garbage in a clear trash bag.* At the same time, ask other volunteers to collect, wash, and dry the washable spoons and bowls.

Questions to ask:
  1. Which group created the most solid waste?
  2. What are the advantages of serving prepackaged, ready-to-eat pudding? Instant pudding?
  3. Many store items are heavily packaged. Why is the packaging an advantage? A disadvantage?

This is why:

   Packaging is beneficial for keeping products fresh and reducing food waste and breakage. But there is a balance. Items that are packaged in single-serving quantities for convenience create excess garbage. One means of reducing garbage is to make wise purchases at the grocery store. Purchases that will create a lot of garbage should be avoided. Garbage can also be reduced by buying the large size of frequently used items.

* After the activity, remove the individual serving cups from the trash. They can be *reused* in Activity 4!

Activity 4: Recycling And Reusing

In advance:
   Ask students to bring to school clean plastic containers that might ordinarily be tossed in the garbage. You can begin your collection with the individual serving cups from Activity 3.

You will need:
one small recycled container   large tray
  for each child   water
potting soil   marigold seeds
sharp, pointed object

What to do:
   Poke a small hole in the bottom of each plastic container. Then have each student partially fill his container with potting soil and plant two or three marigold seeds in his resulting planter. Place all the planters on the tray and sprinkle them with water. Place the tray in a sunny location. Assign a different student to water the planters each day. When the plants have grown to a decent size, send them home as a budding example of recycling and reusing!

Questions to ask:
  1. If these containers had not been brought to school, where do you think they would be now?
  2. How was reducing, reusing, and recycling trash demonstrated?
  3. What are other ways to reduce, reuse, and recycle in school and at home?

This is why:

   Recycling *is the process of reusing or reprocessing a used product to make a new product. In this activity, used containers became planters. If the containers had ended up in the garbage, they probably would have gone to a landfill or an incinerator. However, if the containers had ended up in a plastic recycling plant, they would have been shredded, washed, and melted into pellets. These pellets are then sold to companies that make new plastic items. One of the most surprising uses of recycled plastics is in clothing. Other uses range from making toys and bottles to pencil sharpeners and file cabinets!*

Name _____

The Three Rs

How well are you reducing, recycling, and reusing at school?
Put a tally mark each time you reduce, recycle, or reuse.
Write a description when it is needed.

I **reduced** trash by...

_____ bringing an earth-friendly lunch

_____ using both sides of my paper

_____ using only one paper towel to dry my hands

_____ sharpening my pencil as little as possible

_____

_____

I **recycled**...

_____ lunch items

_____ construction paper

_____ crayons

_____

_____

_____

_____

I **reused**...

_____ a container

_____ buttons, keys, and other manipulatives

_____ magazines, newspapers

_____ fabric

_____

_____

Grand Total: _____

12

Note To Teacher: Encourage students to practice the "Three Rs" in the classroom! Give each student a copy of this page. After several days ask each student to determine how many times he reduced, recycled, and reused in the classroom; then write his total in the Grand Total blank. Repeat the activity as often as desired. Invite interested students to create a checklist to use in their homes.

Keeping The EARTH Alive

Environmental Books For Children

There's no place like home...or is there? Unfortunately in our zeal to build and possess, we have greatly overlooked the importance of preserving our earth's natural resources. Broaden your youngsters' insights into a variety of environmental issues using this selection of old, new, and timeless titles, and the activities that accompany them. *ideas contributed by Kimberly Spring*

Just A Dream

Written & Illustrated by Chris Van Allsburg
Published by Houghton Mifflin Company

One night while lying in bed, Walter wishes he could visit the future—a re he believes will be filled with robots and other amazing inventions. when he falls asleep and his wish comes true, Walter has a frightfully rent vision. And when he awakens the next morning, Walter is inced he must do everything that he can to preserve the earth's ronment.

hank goodness it's not too late for Walter and others to wake up to onmental issues. Read the story a second time, stopping to discuss of Walter's eight environmental encounters. After each encounter, enge students to identify the problem Walter saw, the cause of the lem, and possible solutions. Next have students brainstorm habits that must break to save the environment. For an eye-catching display, list youngsters' suggestions on a large bed-shaped cutout. Mount the ut and the title "Wake Up To The Environment!" on a bulletin board red with black or dark blue paper. Place a supply of large foil stars the display. Each time a student remembers to change a habit for the onment, he attaches a star to the display. The future looks bright!

Farewell To Shady Glade

Written & Illustrated by Bill Peet
Published by Houghton Mifflin Company

When the rumbling noises first began, the woodland creatures of Shady Glade were concerned, but not alarmed. They felt that nothing could ever spoil their perfect home along the wooded creek bank. But when the raccoon scampered to the top of the towering sycamore searching for reassurance, he discovered that he and his friends were doomed. Monstrous machines, leaving nothing but barren earth in their tracks, were headed straight for Shady Glade! With no time to lose, the raccoon contrives a plan to move the small band of inhabitants to a safe place.

In preparation for this follow-up activity, have youngsters discuss the kinds of things the animals in the story needed in their environment to survive. If desired, write their suggestions on the chalkboard. Next divide students into small groups and give each group a section of white bulletin-board paper. Challenge each group to illustrate a desirable environment for a group of animals. Explain that the animals must be included in the illustration and that each environment must have a name. For added appeal, have students complete the artwork using colored pencils, just as Bill Peet did! When the projects are finished, display them for all to see. Several days later, have each student write an environmental tale to accompany one of the illustrations.

The Lorax

Written & Illustrated by Dr. Seuss
Published by Random House

Who else but Dr. Seuss could weave a thought-provoking message into *enchanting tale? The selfish Once-ler decides to mass-produce "thneeds"* *(things we think we need), regardless of the effects on the environment.* *Though warned repeatedly by the Lorax, the Once-ler continues his greedy* *pursuits until nothing is left of the once-pristine land.*

After reading the story aloud, pair students and challenge each twosome develop a plan for how the Once-ler could keep making thneeds without destroying all of the truffula trees. Ask each pair to either illustrate its plan c write a paragraph describing it. Then set aside time for each twosome to sh its plan with its classmates.

For another thought-provoking activity, have students brainstorm a list c present-day thneeds that are harmful to our environment. After writing thei responses on the chalkboard, have students suggest thneed alternatives th. will not harm the environment or create unnecessary waste.

The Paper Bag Prince

Written & Illustrated by Colin Thompson
Published by Alfred A. Knopf, Inc.

When the town dump closes for good, the Paper Bag Prince moves into an *abandoned train car that has been left there. In his new home he finds good uses for* *other people's discards, and he becomes a caretaker of abandoned animals. This wise* *old man knows that nature will gradually reclaim the polluted land and he is doing what* *he can to help with the cleanup.*

As the Paper Bag Prince so vividly points out, much of the trash taking up space in landfills today could be reused. Teach youngsters to recognize reusable items by creating a reusables bin in your classroom. With your students' help, fill the bin with throwaway items that can be reused to create art projects and games. In a larger reusables box, have students place worn or damaged toys, games and clothing that could easily be repaired, and items that they no longer need or want. Make these items available to those who would like them. Or donate the items to a local organization that will distribute the items to needy families.

In addition, start your own classroom recycling center. Label three large boxes "cans," "newspaper," and "plastic." Have youngsters fill the boxes with recyclables from home. Then take the collected materials to the recycling bins in your community.

A River Ran Wild

Written & Illustrated by Lynne Cherry
Published by Harcourt Brace Jovanovich, Publishers

This near-tragic tale is an environmental inspiration. In the beginning the Nash-a- *River (River with the Pebbled Bottom) was an untarnished natural resource. For* *generations, the Nashua people lived alongside and respected this beautiful river. In* *settlers arrived, and soon sawmills and dams began to appear along what was now* *the Nashua River. Next came the Industrial Revolution, bringing with it the rapid grc* *of factories along the river's banks. The resulting waste eventually turned the Nashu* *River into a polluted, ecologically dead waterway. But fortunately this true story is n* *over. Through the efforts of people who were willing to fight for what they believed* *Nashua River has again become the River with the Pebbled Bottom.*

This true tale provides great inspiration for cleaning up the environment. Ask stu to identify places in their neighborhoods that need to be environmentally revitalized invite discussion with the following question: "Do you think you can really make a difference in your neighborhood?" At the end of the discussion, give each child a tag strip. Have the student copy and finish this sentence on his strip: "I can make a diffe in my neighborhood by _____." Have each student take his strip home post it on his family's refrigerator. Then challenge students to put forth the effort to their dreams come true.

The Great Kapok Tree

A Tale Of The Amazon Rain Forest
Written & Illustrated by Lynne Cherry
Published by Harcourt Brace Jovanovich, Publishers

the heart of the Brazilian rain forest, a woodcutter is
ing down a huge kapok tree. Hot and weary, the woodcutter
own to rest and falls asleep at the foot of the tree. As he
s, the creatures who make their homes in the tree emerge
lead with him to not destroy their world.

e kapok tree is one of many trees that are being cut down in
rests throughout the world. The reasons for cutting down
vary. Some people want the wood itself. Others are clearing
or farming, industries, houses, and roads. If the rain forests
ue to be destroyed, creatures, vegetation, and humans will
affected. To begin to understand the losses that could
, write a student-generated list of the forest creatures (from
ok) on a large tree cutout. Add items such as crops
ges, lemons, pineapples, coffee, rice, corn, sugar, bananas),
ng spices (ginger, cloves, cinnamon, mace, nutmeg,
e, cardamom), and medicines (one in four medicines
ns substances derived from rain forest plants). Then display
tout and encourage students to add other appropriate items
list.

share your opinions about the importance of preserving the
rests, have each youngster bring to school a plain white
t. Then, using fabric crayons and/or fabric paint, have each
ster decorate his T-shirt with a message about saving the
rests. Plan to wear the shirts once a month for the remain-
the school year.

Brother Eagle, Sister Sky

Adapted & Illustrated by Susan Jeffers
Published by Dial Books For Young Readers

It was a time of struggle, a time of loss, and a time of devastation. The government in Washington, DC, wished to buy the lands of Chief Seattle's people. Rising to the occasion, Chief Seattle, one of the bravest and most respected chiefs of the Northwest Nations, delivered an impassioned plea for the preservation of his people's land. Susan Jeffers's beautifully illustrated adaptation of Chief Seattle's words sends an environmental message that cannot be ignored.

There's little doubt that your youngsters will want to hear Chief Seattle's message several times over. Explain that the Native American people believed that every creature and part of the earth was sacred—to waste and destroy nature and its wonders was to destroy life itself. In Chief Seattle's lifetime, his people's beliefs were not understood. Find out why your youngsters feel these beliefs will be important in their lifetime. Ask them to consider what condition the earth and its environment might have been in today if others had been heedful of Chief Seattle's words.

Have students consider what they would like to say to Chief Seattle if he were alive. Then have each student decide who he could share a similar message with today. Students may consider family members, the owners of local businesses, their state's governor, or even the president of the United States! Then challenge students to write letters or cards to the people they have chosen. When the cards and letters are in final form, ask each youngster to bring a stamped envelope to school. Arrange for a volunteer to assist youngsters in locating proper addresses and in individually addressing the envelopes. Then place the correspondence in the mail!

Recycling Center

Students will enjoy this center activity over and over again. Leaving the handle intact, trim the top half from a clean, empty, gallon-size milk jug. Using a permanent marker, label each of three Press-on Pockets (available from The Education Center, Inc.) "glass," "paper," and "plastic." Attach each pocket to a different side of the milk jug. Glue pictures of recyclable glass, paper, and plastic items to index cards; then code the backs of the cards for self-checking. Laminate the cards for durability; then place them in the milk jug. A student removes the cards from the milk jug and places each one in its corresponding pocket. After sorting the cards, he checks his work by referring to the programming on the backs of the cards.

Diane Vogel—Gr. 3
W. B. Redding School
Lizella, GA

Creative Recycling

Here's a great way to inspire creativity and promote recycling. Using folded 9" x 1 sheets of construction paper, an assortme of previously used cards, and a variety of arts-and-crafts supplies (such as gift wraj wallpaper, and construction paper scraps; glitter; and markers), have students creat original greeting cards. Students can desi all-occasion cards or cards for specific cel ebrations, then present them to their fam members or friends. When you care enoug you make it yourself!

Suzanne Edmunds
Forest Elementary
Forest, VA

Earth-Friendly Ideas

Recycling Parade

This April celebrate Keep America Beautiful Month with a weeklong recycling project. Ask students to bring clean recyclable items to school; then enlist their help in sorting the items into paper bags, plastic bags, wagons, and other easy-to-transport containers. At the end of the week, line up your students for a recycling parade. Ask each student to carry a portion of the ready-to-recycle items. Student-made banners and posters encouraging others to recycle should also be carried. Then, with a baton held high, quietly march your students through the school. If possible, lead the class to a school or neighborhood recycling facility. Or ask parent volunteers who are willing to transport the items to the nearest facility to meet your students at the end of the parade route. Then load the items into the volunteers' vehicles before returning to class.

Janet Girard—Gr. 2
Pioneer Elementary, Glendale, AZ

Earth Day Math

Head outdoors on Earth Day (April 22) to reinforce measurement skills and promote environmental awareness. Each child needs a paper grocery bag, a ruler, disposable plastic gloves, and a marker. Instruct students to collect trash from the school grounds. Before each item of trash is bagged, a student measures its length in inches and records the measurement on the outside of his bag. After a set amount of time, have each student transfer his trash collection into a trash receptacle, then tally the measurements on his bag to determine how many inches of trash he collected. The message is clear—trash really adds up. As a follow-up, have students suggest ways to take better care of our Earth.

Sheila Asbury—Gr. 2
Hidden Valley Elementary School, Charlotte, NC

The Envelope, Please!

Don't throw away the colorful envelopes that hold greeting cards from loved ones! Gently pull apart the glued flaps of each envelope so that you have a flat piece of paper. The colorful paper can be used for a variety of art projects. Encourage your students to donate used envelopes from home as well.

Christine Kitzmiller—Art Teacher, Sycamore School, Pleasant View, TN

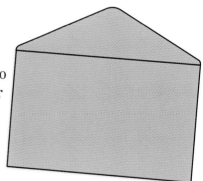

Earth Day Poems

Put your young poets to work writing Earth-friendly poems for Earth Day—and at the same time, reinforce nouns and verbs! On the chalkboard write a student-generated list of nouns that relate to the environment. Then ask the class to brainstorm verbs that relate to the nouns listed. Explain that the verbs must end in *-ing*. Write several of the students' suggestions next to the corresponding nouns. To write an eight-line Earth Day poem, a student writes a title followed by a list of seven noun-verb pairs. His final line is a phrase or sentence that summarizes his topic. Invite students to illustrate and share their prose with their classmates. Repeat the writing activity with any variety of themes or topics.

Zelphia Hutchinson—Gr. 3, Fort Washington Forest Elementary, Fort Washington, MD

Earth Day Party

Celebrate Earth Day (April 22) with a party! Prepare five or six small-group activities that promote caring for the environment like designing Earth Day posters, making paper, planting flower seeds, and designing stationery from scrap paper. Enlist a parent volunteer to supervise each resulting station. To begin the party, send a small group of students to each station. Then, under your direction, have the groups rotate through the stations along an established route. When each group has completed all the activities, serve refreshments. If desired invite students to dress in blue and green for the celebration. Now that's an earth-friendly party!

Candy Whelan—Gr. 3, Garlough Elementary, West St. Paul, MN

Garden On Wheels

Once you've planted those flower seeds at your Earth Day party, a mobile garden is just the thing to make your plants prosper! Place the plants in a toy wagon. When your garden on wheels needs sunlight, simply roll it outside to an unshaded area. Then roll it back in for watering and observation.

Adapted from an idea by Carol Wortham—Gr. 1
Western Elementary School, Newnan, GA

Trash Bag Designs

Learning excitement is in the bag with this fun environmental awareness activity! Give each student a paper bag to label with synonyms for the word trash, such as *litter, refuse, garbage, junk,* etc. After students have added other decorations to their bags, take the class for a walk around your school grounds to pick up litter.

Rachelle Dawson—Gr. 3
Nashua School
Kansas City, MO

Letters From The Future

Environmental issues and geometric shapes provide the backdrop for th futuristic letter-writing activity. To begin, each child creates a futuristic "Geo-Kid." To do this he cuts several geometric shapes from colorful construction paper (provide tagboard tracers if desired). Then he glues hi cutouts in a desired shape onto a 9" x 12" sheet of white construction pap Next, on writing paper, the student writes a letter from "Geo-Kid" to the children of today. In the letter, "Geo-Kid" describes the kinds of things children can do today to help preserve the earth's environment. Mount ea child's completed project on a 12" x 18" sheet of black construction paper before displaying it on a bulletin board for all to see and enjoy.

Rona Mendelson—Gr. 3, Estes McDoniel Elementary, Henderson, NV

R Is For Recycle

Celebrate Earth Day any day by having students make an alphabet booklet of earth-friendly tips. Cut out 26 eight-inch circles from white paper (booklet pages) and two from construction paper (booklet covers). Also cut out each letter of the alphabet from colorful paper. Have each student glue a letter cutout to a white circle and then on the circle write and illustrate an earth-friendly message that begins with her assigned letter. Enlist early finishers to complete leftover booklet pages and to decorate the booklet covers. Then alphabetize the pages and staple them between the covers. There you have it—a world of earth-saving information for your youngsters' reading pleasure!

Always turn off the water while brushing your teeth. Susie

Susie Kapaun—Gr. 2, Leawood Elementary, Littleton, CO

Trash Buster

Over the school year, a large amount of trash can be created from classroom snacks and parties. To reduce the amount of trash your class creates, try this earth-friendly alternative. At the beginning of the year, ask each student to bring a plastic tumbler to school. Have each student decorate and personalize his tumbler using paint pens and permanent markers. Each time beverages are served, use the tumblers; then ask a parent volunteer to wash them. In the spring, have each student grow flower seeds in his tumbler for a Mother's Day gift.

Stephanie Ray Brown—Gr. 1
Newton Parrish, Owensboro, KY

Scrap Art

Construction-paper scraps—they're as valuable as gold to a classroom of young artists! Introduce your students to the works of a famous artist or designer such as Pablo Picasso or Frank Lloyd Wright. After sharing pictures of the artist's work, give each student a supply of paper scraps, a pair of scissors, a piece of art paper, and glue. Have the child cut out and glue the scraps to the paper to create a work of art in the style of the featured artist. Mount the finished projects on poster board or—better yet—old manila file folders. Move over, Monet!

Linda Maxwell
Edgewood Elementary
Birmingham, AL

Ribbon Collages

Have students bring in ribbon scraps from home. (After the holidays is a great time for this activity since there is a plentiful supply of used ribbon from unwrapped gifts.) As a class, discuss the colors, designs, and textures of the ribbons. Then give each child several pieces of ribbon, scissors, glue, and piece of art paper. Demonstrate the collage technique and ways that students can glue the ribbons on their papers to create interesting effects (such as scrunching the ribbon, using a pencil to create a ripple effect, curling the ribbon with scissors, etc.). The results of this creative recycling project make for an eyecatching display!

Karen Megay-Nespoli, Public School 87, Queens, Middle Village, NY

Top This!

Before you toss a dried-up marker or an empty bottle of food coloring in the trash, remove the colorful plastic top. Recycle these to use as:

- tokens for board games
- manipulatives for color sorting or counting
- materials for making finger puppets
- nonstandard units for measuring activities

Karen Spooner—Gr. 1
Georgian Heights School
Columbus, OH

A Trash-Free Lunch

Celebrate Earth Day with a monthlong project that your students can really sink their teeth into! Every Friday in April, challenge your class to bring trash-free lunches to school. The lunches should be packed with as many reusable items as possible. (For example, students can pack cloth napkins instead of paper ones or bring their lunches in reusable containers instead of paper bags.) Send home a parent letter explaining the project along with a copy of the "A Closer Look At Your Lunch" form below. For each child, staple four copies of the form below in a folder. Each Friday, head outdoors for a "recycling picnic." At the end of the picnic, have each child evaluate his lunch using a checklist in his folder. By the end of this hands-on recycling project, your students will be pros at eliminating lunchtime waste!

Rose Marie Gonzales—Gr. 2
Leonelo Gonzalez School
McAllen, TX

Name_____

A Closer Look At Your Lunch

Put a check (√) beside each item that is in your lunch.

Remember: Your goal is to check as many "trash-free" boxes as possible.

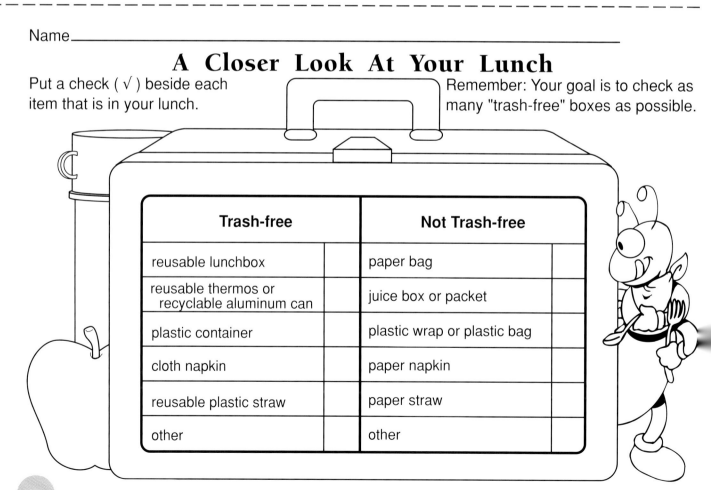

Trash-free		Not Trash-free	
reusable lunchbox		paper bag	
reusable thermos or recyclable aluminum can		juice box or packet	
plastic container		plastic wrap or plastic bag	
cloth napkin		paper napkin	
reusable plastic straw		paper straw	
other		other	

Invite students to lend a hand in preserving the earth! Each student colors and cuts out a copy of the earth pattern on page 22. The student also traces one hand atop a sheet of colorful construction paper; then he cuts out and programs the resulting shape with an earth-friendly tip. Mount the hand cutouts around a large globe cutout. Display a snapshot of each child atop his earth cutout. The title says it all—"Earth: It's In Our Hands!"

Mary Jo Kampschnieder—Gr. 2, Howells Community Catholic, Howells, NE

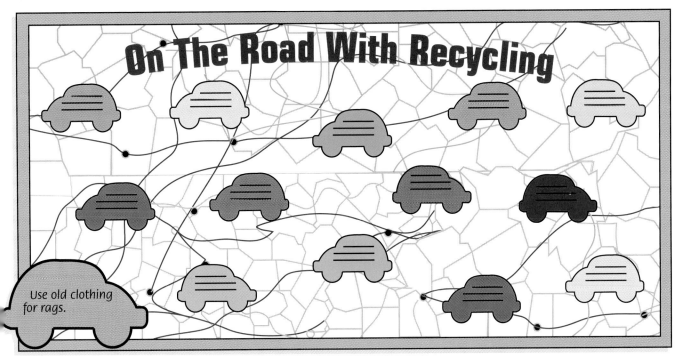

Take a recycling road trip! Cover a display area with discarded road maps and mount the title. Using the pattern on page 22, duplicate a supply of colorful construction-paper cars. Each student cuts out a pattern and writes a recycling suggestion on the resulting car shape. Ask each child to share his recycling tip before you mount his cutout on the display. Vroooom!

Gina Parisi—Gr. 2, Demarest School, Bloomfield, NJ

Patterns

Use with "On The Road With Recycling" on page 21.

Use with "Earth: It's In Our Hands!" on page 21.

Background For The Teacher
Ecology

Some of the major problems confronting our planet today include air and water pollution, acid rain, disappearing wildlife and forests, garbage, the greenhouse effect, and the ozone hole. Difficult as these problems are, there are many things that can be done—even by children—to alleviate them.

Recycle! Plastic, aluminum, paper, cardboard, and glass can be recycled. The energy savings from recycling just one glass bottle will burn a 100-watt light bulb for four hours! The energy saved from recycling one aluminum can will run a television set for three hours!

Conserve water! Even though two-thirds of the earth is ocean, it's too salty to drink. We need to protect our fresh drinking water. Turn off the water when you brush your teeth. Take showers instead of baths. Don't pour paint or oil on the ground. These substances pollute the groundwater that you drink.

Make room for animals! A birdhouse, summer birdbath, or winter feeder will welcome birds. Cultivate plants that birds like to eat, such as sunflowers. Don't buy items made out of ivory, tortoise shell, coral, reptile skins, or exotic cat skins. These products come from endangered animals or plants.

Save the trees! Trees absorb carbon dioxide in the air. Plant a tree in your yard. Take good care of the trees you already have. Recycle paper products so fewer trees will be cut. It does make a difference. If everyone in the United States recycled their Sunday paper, 500,000 trees could be saved every week.

Conserve energy! Ride your bike or walk when possible. Turn off unused appliances and lights. Keep heat in your house by closing curtains and blinds on cold nights. Plug leaks around doors and windows. Open and close the refrigerator quickly.

How To Use Page 25

1. Discuss things that can be recycled.
2. Ask students to contribute items that can be recycled. Place an assortment of these items in a bin. Put the bin in a learning center along with the graph on page 25 and some crayons.
3. Have students (individually, in pairs, or in small groups) graph the recyclables contained in the bin.

Variation

Provide several bins filled with recyclables. Have each of several small groups of students graph the recyclable items in a different bin. Then have the groups compare and discuss their results.

Teacher Reference Books
Environmental Awareness

Rain Forest Secrets
Written & Illustrated by Arthur Dorros
Published by Scholastic Inc.

Recycled Songs Book And Cassette
Written by Don Cooper & Illustrated by R. W. Alley
Published by Random House, Inc.

My Recyclable Record

Color the blocks to show how many pieces you found.

| glass | plastic | paper | aluminum | cardboard |

Materials Needed For Each Child

pencil, scissors, crayons or paint, stapler, glue

How To Use Pages 26–27

1. Reproduce pages 26 and 27 on construction paper or tagboard.
2. Have students read page 27. Discuss earth's ecological problems as well as ways that youngsters can contribute to their solutions.
3. Instruct students to color or paint the circular design (page 27) and cut it out.
4. Have students cut on the pattern outline on page 26. Provide extra sheets of manuscript paper that have been cut to match the outline on page 26. Staple one or two of these sheets beneath each student's page 26 cutout.
5. Have each student glue his circular cutout to the stapled pages as indicated.
6. Have each student write his name and write several things he plans to do to help save the earth.

Glue bottom of circle here.

My name is

I can help the earth. I can…

Listen and do.

The earth is my beautiful home.

I can care for it.

Poster Props

Fold.

A

How To Use Pages 28 And 29 To Make A Stand-Up Earth Day Poster

1. In advance gather a photocopy of each child's school picture. Reproduce pages 28 and 29 onto card stock for each child. Prepare page 29 for student use by cutting the small circle along the broken line using an X-acto® knife.
2. Distribute pages 28 and 29 to each child and ask her to cut out her poster and two props along the heavy solid outlines.
3. Have each student tape her school photo to the back of the Earth Day poster so that her face shows through the circle. Ask her to color the poster as desired.
4. Encourage each child to share a way that she can help take care of the earth. Ask her to write her name and idea at the bottom of her poster.
5. To complete the poster, have each child fold and glue the gray portions of her poster props to the back edges of her poster. Then have her connect the props by gluing as indicated.

Poster Variation

To add interest to the posters, provide plant- and animal-shaped sponge cutouts. Have each child dip each sponge in brightly colored tempera paint, then stamp the shape onto black construction paper. After the paint has dried, have her cut out each shape, leaving a small black border. Have each student glue the bottom edges of the shapes along the top arc of her poster.

Fold.

Fold.

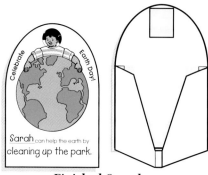

Finished Sample

Glue
A
here.

Fold.

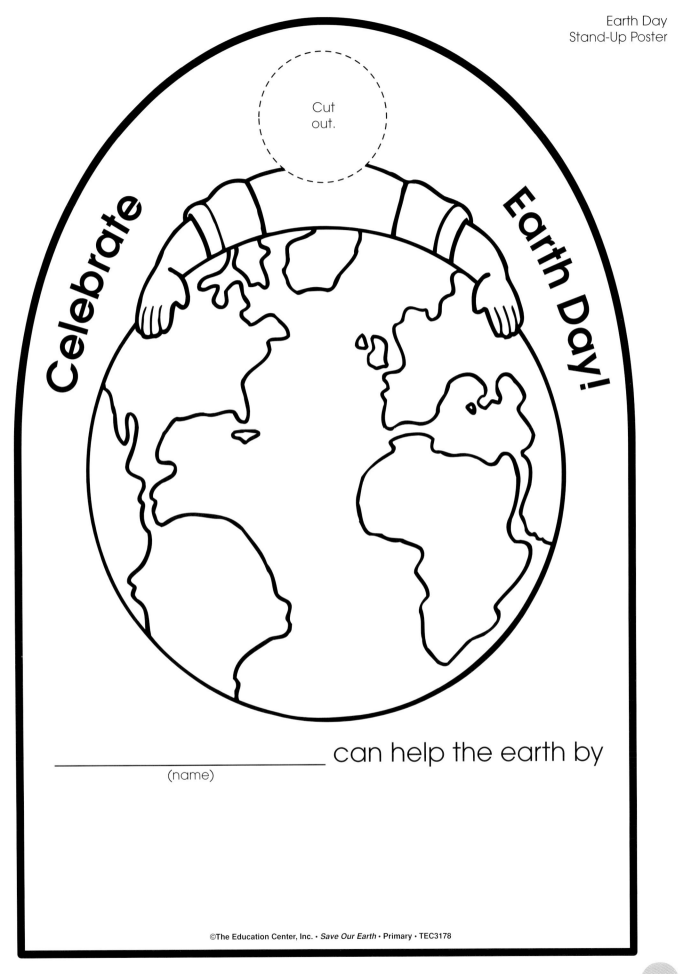

Cut
out.

Celebrate

Earth Day!

_____ can help the earth by
(name)

Background For The Teacher
Recycling

There is a huge problem facing our country today—what to do with all the garbage. For years landfills, dumps, and incinerators have handled wastes. But landfills are closing because they are filled with slowly decomposing trash, such as aluminum and plastic, that can take up to 500 years to break down—and glass that *never* decomposes. And new landfills take up space that could be used for other purposes. Landfills and incinerators also pose health risks because harmful chemicals are released into the environment through leaching and burning.

The three Rs—*reduce, reuse,* and *recycle*—represent the best answers to garbage reduction. *Reducing* means lessening the amount of trash through wise buying of items with little packaging. *Reusing* means finding new uses for items such as plastic or glass containers, clothes, and toys that would normally be thrown out. *Recycling* is the process of turning something that is old or used into something that can be used again.

Glass, aluminum, tin, paper, and plastic can all be recycled. Glass is 100 percent recyclable into new containers or into ingredients used in bricks, reflective paints, and street paving. Recycled aluminum may be made into new cans—using 95 percent less energy than those made from scratch. Recycled paper becomes new paper, tissue, or paper towels. Milk jugs and soda bottles are the most commonly recycled plastic. They may be made into new carpet fibers, rope, or trash cans. Many people are now *composting*, or recycling organic garbage. This cuts down on the space used in landfills and produces rich fertilizers.

Recycling is a good alternative to simply throwing out trash because it reduces the amount of pollution that is produced, saves energy, and saves natural resources.

Materials Needed For Each Child
—copies of pages 31–33
—crayons
—a pencil
—scissors

You Will Need
—a stapler

How To Use Pages 31–33 To Make A Recycling Booklet

1. Give each student a copy of each duplicated page. Have each student cut on the heavy, solid outlines surrounding each page.
2. Ask each student to sequence the pages, then align the left edges. Staple each student's booklet together along the left edge.
3. Introduce students to recycling by reading the background information (see "Background For The Teacher: Recycling"). Or read aloud one or more of the books listed in the related literature section.
4. To complete the booklet cover (page 31), have each student write her name in the space provided and then complete the blank face.
5. Read each poem on the remaining booklet pages (pages 31–33) one at a time. After reading each poem, guide students in discussing and completing the booklet page.

Teacher's Reference
Recycling
Earth-Friendly Toys
Written & Illustrated by George Pfiffn
Published by John Wiley & Sons, Inc.

Related Literature
Recycling
Recycle! A Handbook For Kids
Written & Illustrated by Gail Gibbons
Published by Little, Brown
    and Company

Recycling
Written by Joan Kalbacken &
    Emilie U. Lepthien
Published by Childrens Press®

Here Comes The Recycling Truck!
Written & Illustrated by Meyer Seltze
Published by Albert Whitman
    & Company

*The Berenstain Bears Don't Pollute
    (Anymore)*
Written by Stan & Jan Berenstain
Published by Random House, Inc.

Recycling Sam wants you to know,
Protecting the earth is the way to go.
If you want to see pollution erased,
Reduce, **recycle**, and **reuse** the waste.

The three Rs to help the earth are:

_____

_____

_____

Recycling Sam And

_____
(student's name)

To The Rescue

1

3

Sam's mom reads the news each day,
And afterward Sam is sure to say,
"Paper is reusable, as everyone knows.
Stack up the papers; we'll recycle those."

Another way to save paper is _____

_____

2

Aluminum cans and aluminum foil
Break down slowly in the soil.
Save your aluminum waste and then
Toss it in the recycling bin.

Write yes or no for each sentence.

_____ Aluminum breaks down quickly
       in the soil.

_____ Aluminum should be recycled.

Metal

32

©The Education Center, Inc. • *Save Our Earth* • Primary • TEC3178

Recycling with nature is a good thing to do
To cut down on waste and help fertilize, too.
Parents and children can all work together
To keep the earth beautiful now and forever.

I can help make a beautiful earth by

When you empty the juice from the bottle,
Will you be someone we all wish to model?
Like Recycling Sam, will you use it again
And work toward being earth's best friend?

I can use an empty juice bottle to make

Paper   Glass   Metal   Plastic

Metal

Glass

•••••Recycling Sam To The Rescue•••••

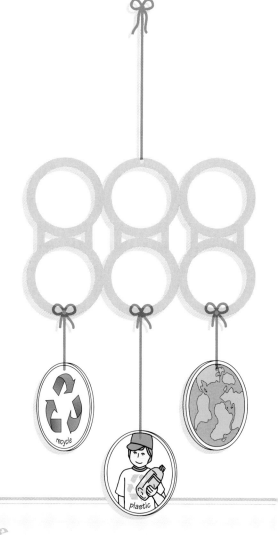

Materials Needed For Each Child

— one copy of page 35
— three clean, plastic tops (such as tops from yogurt, frosting, or play dough containers)
— plastic six-pack soda-can holder
— a hole puncher (or access to a hole puncher)
— two 14" lengths of string
— two 10" lengths of string
— crayons
— scissors
— glue

You Will Need

— a sharp object (a pair of sharp scissors or the pointed end of a compass will work well)

How To Use Page 35 To Make A Trash-To-Treasure Mobile

1. In advance ask each student to bring three plastic tops and a plastic soda-can holder from home. Use a sharp, pointed object to carefully make a hole (large enough for a piece of string to easily glide through) near the edge of each plastic top.
2. Have each student punch three holes on one long side of his plastic soda-can holder—one on the end, one in the middle, and one on the other end. Have him punch one hole in the middle of the other long side of the plastic soda-can holder.
3. Assist each student in tying one of the 14-inch lengths of string through the center hole in the top length of his soda-can holder. This will serve as a hanger for the mobile.
4. Have each student thread a length of string through each of his three lids. Then help him tie each length of string through a hole on the soda-can holder, using the longest string in the middle hole.
5. Have each student color and cut out the designs on page 35. Then instruct the student to glue a design to the front and back of each lid.

Variation

Instead of using the patterns on page 35, a beautiful mobile can also be made by having each student cut designs from used wrapping paper or greeting cards, and then having her glue them to her lids.

Name _____

Trash-To-Treasure Mobile

Color.
Cut.
Glue.

How To Use Page 37

1. Provide a copy of page 37 for each student.
2. Allow each student to take the page home. Ask each student to color in the appropriate space for each action that he completes.
3. After a planned amount of time, present each student who completes a predetermined number of items with a copy of the award below.

Variation

Present each student who participates with a small package of seeds or a sapling that she can take home and plant.

Award

You've reduced, reused, and recycled, too.
So this award is presented to you!

_____
(student's name)

is a friend of the earth!

©The Education Center, Inc. • *Save Our Earth* • Primary • TEC3178

Raring To Recycle!

Do your part to help the earth!
Color in a space after you have completed that activity.

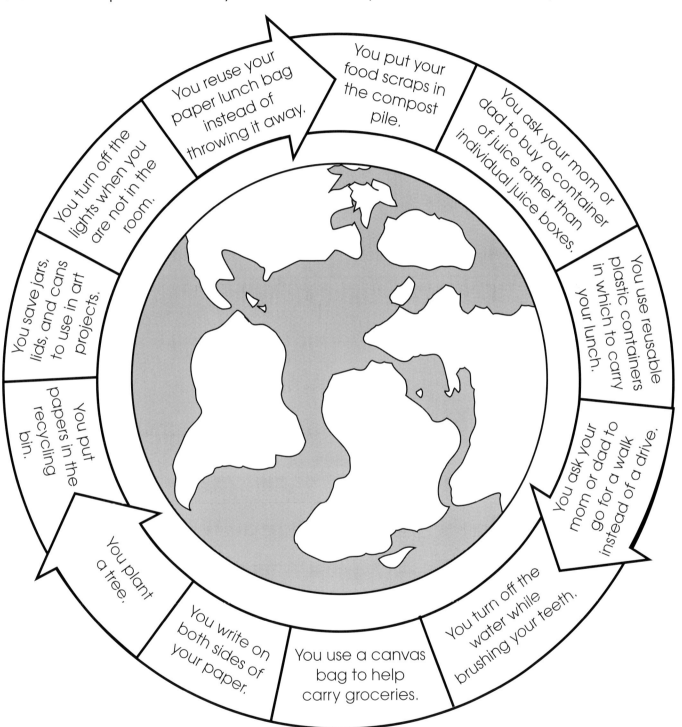

You reuse your paper lunch bag instead of throwing it away.

You put your food scraps in the compost pile.

You ask your mom or dad to buy a container of juice rather than individual juice boxes.

You turn off the lights when you are not in the room.

You use reusable plastic containers in which to carry your lunch.

You save jars, lids, and cans to use in art projects.

You ask your mom or dad to go for a walk instead of a drive.

You put papers in the recycling bin.

You turn off the water while brushing your teeth.

You plant a tree.

You write on both sides of your paper.

You use a canvas bag to help carry groceries.

Background For The Teacher

Earth Day

Earth Day was first observed around the world on April 22, 1970. The theme of this global celebration of our planet was "Give Earth A Chance." The United Nations joined with countries around the world in focusing on what humanity could do to reclaim the purity of air, water, and natural environments. Although the first Earth Day was celebrated in 1970, the April date has been an important one for the earth for more than a century.

April 22 is the traditional date when Arbor Day, a celebration of trees and living things, is observed. Arbor Day began in Nebraska in 1872. Julius Morton, a newspaper publisher and politician, recognized that planting trees would enrich the dry Nebraska soil. He lobbied the Nebraska legislature to establish April 10 as a day for planting trees. When he died, his friends in the legislature changed the date of Arbor Day to April 22, Morton's birthday. Soon other states began observing Arbor Day on April 22 as well.

Today Earth Day is observed worldwide on a variety of dates, although the two most common ones are April 22 and March 20 or 21, the day of the vernal equinox.

Extension Activity

Caring for the earth is an ongoing project. Each week set aside time for interested students to describe for their classmates how they have cared for the earth during the previous week. Conclude the sharing session by presenting each child who shared with a completed copy of the Friend Of The Earth award on this page.

Answer Key For Page 39

The pictures that accompany sentences 1, 5, 6, and 7 should be colored. Sentences 2, 3, 4, and 8 should be rewritten. Answers will vary but may include:

2—*Use both sides of a sheet of paper.*
3—*Ride a bike or walk whenever possible.*
4—*Do not leave the water running while you brush your teeth.*
8—*Never litter!*

Awards   Use with the "Extension Activity" on this page.

_____
is a
Friend Of The Earth
because _____

_____

_____

Keep up
the good work!

Date: _____
Signed: _Earth Man_

_____
is a
Friend Of The Earth
because _____

_____

_____

Keep up
the good work!

Date: _____
Signed: _Earth Man_

Name_____

Earth Day Decisions

Read each suggestion below.
If the suggestion is good for the earth, color the picture.

1. Turn off the TV when no one is watching it.		5. Always recycle.	
2. Use only one side of a sheet of paper.		6. Carry your lunch in a reusable container.	
3. Ride in a car instead of riding a bike or walking.		7. Respect the habitats of wildlife.	
4. Leave the water running while you brush your teeth.		8. A little bit of littering is OK.	

In each box, write the number of a suggestion from above that is not earth-friendly.
On the lines, rewrite the suggestion so that it is good for the earth.

[ ] _____
    _____

[ ] _____
    _____

[ ] _____
    _____

[ ] _____
    _____

Bonus Box: On the back of this paper, draw and color a picture that illustrates one suggestion that you rewrote.

Materials Needed For Each Child

crayons
scissors
glue
12" x 2" construction paper strip (one per student)
one copy of page 41

How To Use Page 41

As a group, brainstorm a list of things kids can do to help clean up the Earth and reduce the amount of trash in the environment. Then have students complete their reproducibles using the directions at right.

Directions For The Student

1. Color the pictures of things Earth Kids do.
2. Cut along the dotted line at the bottom of the page.
3. Cut out the pictures you colored.
4. Glue the colored pictures on the construction paper strip.
5. Cut the slits near the window on the Earth Kids' clubhouse.
6. Insert the strip through the slits.
7. Slide the strip to show what Earth Kids do.

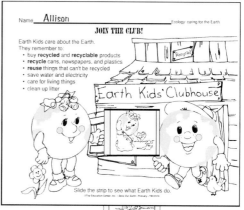

Answer Key For Page 42

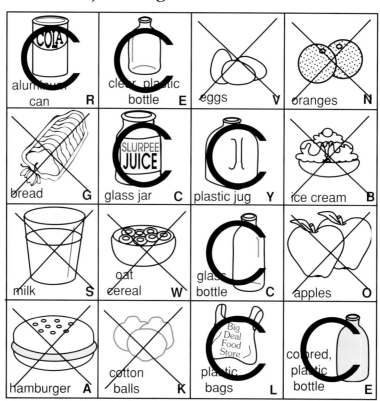

Answer to riddle: They recycle!

Join The Club!

Earth Kids care about the Earth.
They remember to:

- buy **recycled** and **recyclable** products
- **recycle** cans, newspapers, and plastics
- **reuse** things that can't be recycled
- save water and electricity
- care for living things
- clean up litter

Slide the strip to see what Earth Kids do.

©The Education Center, Inc. • *Save Our Earth* • Primary • TEC3178

Color the things Earth Kids do.
Cut and glue those pictures on a strip of paper.

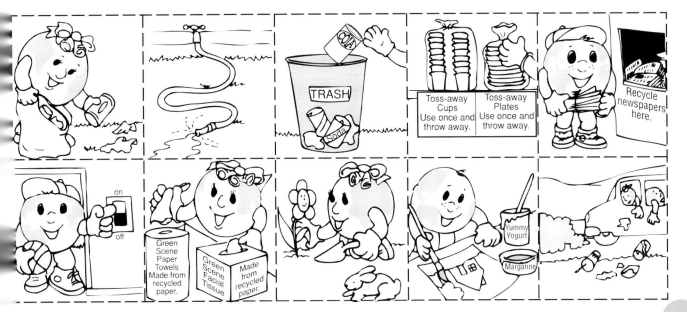

Name _____

A Treasure Hunt

The Earth is full of treasures! Some of the Earth's treasures are **renewable**. New ones grow to take their place. Renewable treasures come from plants and animals.

Other treasures are **nonrenewable**. When these treasures are taken from the Earth, they cannot be replaced for many, many years. Nonrenewable treasures come from rocks and minerals. Products made from oil, like plastics and gasoline, are nonrenewable, too.

Help the Earth Kids find the path to save the Earth's nonrenewable treasures.

Color the **nonrenewable** treasures.
Draw an **X** on the **renewable** treasures.

 Start

Follow the path.
Find the letters in the colored boxes.
Write them in the spaces below.

Finish

How do Earth Kids save nonrenewable treasures?

They __ __ __ __ __ __ __ !

Name _____   Earth Kids: Problem solving

Earth Kids' Pledge

The Earth Kids' Pledge
Recycle what you can.
Reuse what you can't recycle.
Reduce the amount of trash you throw away.
Respect the Earth.

Think of ways Earth Kids can carry out their pledge.
Write what the Earth Kids could do.

Earl finds an aluminum can in his yard.
Earl _____
_____ .

Earlene can't recycle a Styrofoam® egg carton. Earlene _____
_____ .

Earl's dad has papers that have only been used on one side. Earl _____
_____
_____ .

Earlene's friends throw candy wrappers on the playground. Earlene _____
_____
_____ .

Write a sentence to tell about something you can do to show you are keeping the Earth Kids' Pledge.

I can _____

_____ .

Draw and color a picture of what you can do on the back of this sheet.

Award

Duplicate this award on white construction paper for any student who completes a predetermined number of the activities on the contract.

To make a necklace award, have the student color and cut out a copy of the award. Then glue it inside a plastic, margarine or cream cheese lid, and punch a hole near the top. Thread a length of yarn or curling ribbon through the hole and tie the loose ends.

Pattern

_____

**is an official member
of the**

Earth Kids' Club

©The Education Center, Inc.

completed necklace award

Katie
is an official member
of the
Earth Kids' Club

Answer Key For Page 47

<u>Yes</u>	<u>No</u>
ⓑ	k
a	ⓘ
ⓖ	p
ⓒ	s
o	ⓐ
ⓡ	m

The paper four people use in one year weighs about as much as a **big car**.

Name _____

Earth Kids' Contract

Become a member of the Earth Kids Club! Color each shape as you complete the activity.

4. Make a poster about recycling. Use the blank side of a cereal box panel.

6. Cut and staple used paper to make a notepad. Decorate each sheet with a stamp or drawing.

3. Make a collage using pictures of recyclables.

10. Pack a trash-free lunch. Put food in containers that can be used again. Pack a cloth napkin.

2. Decorate a cardboard box to hold recyclables.

5. Invent an indoor game using recyclables. Play it with a friend.

9. Trade an old toy with a friend instead of throwing it away.

8. Write a thank-you note to a person who cares for the Earth.

1. Go to a grocery store. Make a list of five products that are packaged in or made from recycled materials.

7. Decorate an old pillowcase to create a reusable shopping bag.

Extension Activity
Earth Kids' Classroom Handbook

Your students are sure to enjoy creating an "Earth Kids' Handbook" for your classroom. Duplicate one copy of the booklet page below for each child. Have each child draw and color a picture of something she can do to help improve the environment. Then have her write a sentence or two about her drawing.

To make covers for the handbook, paint two, six-inch paper plates to resemble the Earth. When the covers have dried, use a permanent black marker to add facial features and the title "Earth Kids' Handbook" to the front cover. Staple the students' completed pages between the decorated covers.

Pattern

Name _____

A Club Project

The Earth Kids recycle newspaper. Newspaper is made from trees. Recycling newspaper helps save trees. Recycled newspaper can be used to make cereal boxes, construction paper, and paper egg cartons.

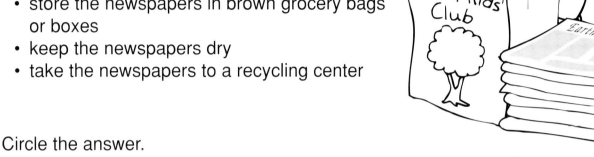

To recycle used newspapers, the Earth Kids:
- collect clean newspapers
- store the newspapers in brown grocery bags or boxes
- keep the newspapers dry
- take the newspapers to a recycling center

Circle the answer.

	Yes	No
Recycling newspapers saves trees.	b	k
Newspapers should be kept wet.	a	i
Newspapers can be stored in brown grocery bags.	g	p
Cereal boxes can be made from recycled newspapers.	c	s
Newspapers that have paint on them can be recycled.	o	a
Construction paper can be made from recycled newspaper.	r	m

Write the letters you circled in the blanks below.

The paper four people use in one year weighs about as much as a

___ ___ ___ ___   ___ ___ ___ .

Name _____

Rain Forest Problems

The Earth Kids have learned that
rain forests are big, wet woodlands.
They help make the earth's weather.
They help make our air.
Many plants and animals live there.
People are cutting down rain forests.
Soon the rain forests will be gone.

Read each box.
Add or subtract.

3 tall bugs go by. 3 more bugs go by. How many in all? 3+3=6 [6] bugs	8 birds rest in a tree. 3 fly away. How many are left? [ ] birds	9 snakes sun on a rock. 1 more comes over. How many in all? [ ] snakes
2 red flowers grow. 8 blue flowers grow. How many in all? [ ] flowers	10 trees are by the creek. 7 are cut down. How many are left? [ ] trees	4 frogs hop by. 3 more hop by. How many in all? [ ] frogs
3 monkeys chatter. 5 more chatter. How many in all? [ ] monkeys	7 mice run into a hole. 2 more run in. How many in all? [ ] mice	5 ants are working. 2 go home. How many are left? [ ] ants